Natural Inspirations

JORI JONES

Balboa Press books may be ordered through booksellers or by contacting:

Balboa Press
A Division of Hay House
1663 Liberty Drive
Bloomington, IN 47403
www.balboapress.com
1 (877) 407-4847

ISBN: 978-1-4525-1700-1 (sc)
ISBN: 978-1-4525-1701-8 (e)

Library of Congress Control Number: 2014911786

Printed in the United States of America.

Balboa Press rev. date: 10/31/2014

BALBOA.
PRESS
A DIVISION OF HAY HOUSE

This book is dedicated to all who seek to bring peace to the planet, especially those who serve in the armed forces. May God keep you safe in all that you do. I would like to thank Chuck for his encouragement, love and for the many adventures we have shared. Also, to Buddy Bear for just being himself and for showing me what truly unconditional love is. He is an example of what that can come from tragedy and disaster if all intentions are for good!

It is my hope that in reading my verses, thoughts and observations, you will feel inspired to truly love and embrace this amazing planet and the life we've all been gifted. This is a collection of writing that I have done over forty-plus years and photos that I have taken a little more recently.

Love each day; love all you meet and drink in everything around you. I hope too that you will appreciate that this earth is a very special place indeed, and that there is beauty around you no matter where you are.

May God bless you with peace and abundance of spirit! Celebrate each day!

Mountain Goat, Logan Pass, Glacier Nat. Park, Montana

Look for the highest place for your spirit to dwell.
Find your power there and allow no one to
take that power from you.
It is divine and given only to you.

Hidden Lake Overlook, Glacier Nat. Park, Montana

Table Rock State Park, Missouri

Remember the gifts the Universe has already given to You.
They are not given lightly.
All of what you need, you already possess; just pause to remember.

Au Sable River, Northern Michigan

Fall Creek, Umpqua Valley, Oregon

**Allow nature to remind you that it ebbs and flows;
it is gentle and forceful in order to balance itself in the
large eternal picture.
Allowing yourself to do the same is loving and respecting you.
When you love and respect yourself you have the same
to freely give away, and that is a gentle balance of
wonderful energy in all worlds.**

Multnomah Falls, Oregon

Petroglyphs, Chaco Culture Nat. Historic Park, New Mexico

Accept that you are a part of the plan of the Universe and eternal time.

Grand Canyon Nat. Park, Arizona

Chaco Culture Nat. Historic Park, New Mexico

Be thankful for everything.
We came into this world with nothing and we take
nothing with us when we leave it.

Chaco Culture Nat Historic Park, New Mexico

Highline Trail, Glacier National Park, Montana

**It is not our place to judge the path of others
but to bless the path they are on.**

Lake McDonald, Glacier Nat. Park, Montana

Serviceberry blossoms, Montana

Be at peace with yourself and awaken your senses to all that is here; all that is life. Be aware of the earthy perfume of the soil, the sweet songs of birds and soft rustling of leaves in the breeze.

Great Smoky Mountains Nat. Park, Tennessee

Chapel at Hartwick Pines State Park, Michigan

Begin each day with prayer and thanks.

Fall Aspens at Two Medicine, Glacier Nat. Park, Montana

Bull moose, Many Glacier, Glacier Nat. Park, Montana

**Love all creatures
great and small.**

Leopard Frog, Lake McDonald, Glacier Nat. Park, Montana

Grand-dogs, Ace and Deuce enjoying a beautiful day

**Perhaps if we all behaved more like our beloved pets,
happy to just be, and content with the very basics, the
world would be a more peaceful place.**

Buddy Bear with a happy smile near Glacier Park, Montana

Joplin, Missouri after EF-5 tornado May 22, 2011

When focused on a noble task, the little annoyances in life do not seem to matter. Perhaps we should always try then to focus on what really matters.

Emergency shelter for Joplin Humane Society
with volunteers Tiffany and Shannon

Grant Farm Island, Florida

**It is amazing to think that if you stand outside and look
at the moon and stars, there is virtually nothing between you and the Universe. There
is nothing to stop us from
becoming what we see above and around us, for the
Universe is inside us all and anything is possible!**

Ft. Mc Allister State Park, Georgia

Antelope Canyons, Page, Arizona

**Love yourself and don't be afraid to use the gifts
you were born with. This will expand your spirit.**

Near Moab, Utah

Rufous hummingbird, Montana

**Every day in every life is more precious than any jewel; it <u>is</u> life.
So live each day joyfully!**

Spring rainbow, Montana

Dolphin Research Center, Grassy Key, Florida

Show your zest for life, and every person you meet will feel it also.

Dolphin Research Center, Grassy Key, Florida

Buddy Bear on adoption day in Joplin

Buddy Bear as shop dog
with friend, Mark

Each act of kindness goes out much further than we might ever realize.

Teddy the rescued Therapy Dog

Lake McDonald, Glacier Nat. Park, Montana

God softly nudged my eyes to open, just in time to see
Perfection in the sunrise He created just for me!
The masterpiece was fleeting,
Its soft palette did unfold.
A few moments with God's perfection
Is worth hours to the soul!

Confluence of Missouri and Niobrara Rivers, Niobrara, Nebraska

Monument Valley, Utah

The Universe effortlessly allows harmonious moments of balance and beauty to just happen; like the ancient rock sentinels, whose power is emitted just by being.
It just is.
That same kind of power is ours to acknowledge and absorb if we accept it.
All things are possible to those who transcend such power within themselves.

The Watchman, Zion Nat. Park, Utah

Ferns on Avalanche Trail, Glacier Nat. Park, Montana

Tranquility

Shafts of
Sunlight
Filter
Through
Branches
And leaves.
The moss   below   is
Grateful   for   each
Drop   it
Receives.
Emerald   ferns   guide
The path
And stars   guide   the trees.
Nature's silent host
Beckons us to stay
as the forest rests,
nurtured,
at the end
of the day.

Avalanche Lake Trail, Glacier Nat. Park, Montana

Teton Nat. Park, Wyoming

**Stay close to the Earth Mother.
She embraces us and we are a part of her.**

Birch trees, Glacier Nat. Park, Montana

Wild Columbine, Glacier Nat. Park, Montana

**When we love our own spirit and attend to its needs
we are loving God.
For our spirit was made by Him, and has been only
waiting for our surrender, to allow miracles to
happen each and every day.**

Long Key State Park, Florida

Sperry Glacier Trail, Glacier Nat. Park, Montana

**Be gentle with all you meet.
Treat them the way you would like to be treated.**

Juvenile Rufous hummingbird, Montana

Lake McDonald morning mist, Glacier Nat. Park, Montana

A soft, mystic air
Binds earth with sky.
Ancient vapors rise,
Made visible to the eye.
There is a sense of presence
And spirit you can feel,
As we search for life's answers
It's an energy that's real.
The balance of just being
And peace of the soul;
Inspiration for living,
At one with the whole.

Hungry Horse Reservoir, Hungry Horse, Montana

Logan Pass, Glacier Nat. Park, Montana

Sunset at Grant Farm Island, Florida

May the beauty of the Earth fill you with peace.

Jori has always had a love of nature. Hiking and being outdoors has been her way of finding peace and has inspired her to share her thoughts and photography. Jori has one daughter and two grand-dogs, and she lives near Glacier National Park in northwest Montana.

Printed in the United States
By Bookmasters